T0071046

John Rutter
CAROLS

O HOLY NIGHT

Thirteen sacred carols and Christmas hymns for mixed voices

EDITED AND ARRANGED
BY JOHN RUTTER

MUSIC DEPARTMENT

OXFORD
UNIVERSITY PRESS

PREFACE

O HOLY NIGHT presents thirteen of the finest and best-loved sacred carols and Christmas hymns in choral arrangements which may be performed either separately or else as a sequence (with or without readings and prayers) forming a complete Christmas service or concert.

Each arrangement is complete in itself, so the suggested sequence (shown with readings and prayers on p. 58) can be shortened or altered to suit the needs of different choirs and occasions.

Five Christmas hymns are included, in arrangements for choir, congregation/audience, and organ or orchestra. The opening hymn, *O come, O come, Emmanuel,* is suitable for use as a processional introit. Five carols are arranged for unaccompanied choir, and four for choir with piano, organ, or orchestra.

Instrumentation for the accompanied items is listed at the foot of their first pages. The hymns are scored for full orchestra, but any of the woodwind, brass and percussion may be omitted if organ is available. The carols are scored for small orchestra. All the accompaniments may satisfactorily be played by piano or organ alone.

Companion volumes of the John Rutter Carols:

JOY TO THE WORLD! (fifteen sacred carols and Christmas hymns)
WE WISH YOU A MERRY CHRISTMAS (twelve secular carols and Christmas songs)

Note:
Orchestral scores and parts are available from Oxford University Press.

CONTENTS

Carols suitable for unaccompanied singing are marked thus: *

TITLE PAGE

O come, O come, Emmanuel 1
French 15th-cent. arr. John Rutter

*Angels we have heard on high 4
French trad. arr. John Rutter

Angels, from the realms of glory 9
Henry Smart arr. John Rutter

*Ding dong! merrily on high 12
French 16th-cent. arr. Charles Wood

*What child is this? 13
English trad. arr. John Rutter

Good Christian men, rejoice 16
German 14th-cent. arr. John Rutter

The first Nowell 21
English trad. arr. John Rutter

Away in a manger 26
J.R. Murray arr. John Rutter

O holy night 30
(Cantique de Noël)
Adolphe Adam arr. John Rutter

*Joy to the world 43
Lowell Mason

*Three kings of Orient 44
J.H. Hopkins arr. John Rutter

Go, tell it on the mountain 46
American folk song arr. John Rutter

Hark! the herald angels sing 54
Mendelssohn arr. John Rutter

A service of readings and carols 58

O COME, O COME, EMMANUEL

for Mixed Voices, S. A. T. B., Congregation, with Organ*

Words 18th Century
Tr. J. M. NEALE

Melody from 15th-century
French Processional
arranged by JOHN RUTTER

In measured tempo, solemn (♩=63)

VERSES 1 and 4

CHOIR and CONGREGATION**

f

1. O come, O come, Em - ma - nu - el, And ran-som cap-tive Is - ra -
4. O come, O come, thou Lord of might, Who to thy tribes, on Si - nai's

Organ Man.

f

Ped.

-el, That mourns in lone-ly ex - ile here Un - til the Son of God ap -
height, In an - cient times didst give the law In cloud and ma-jes - ty, and

ff

-pear.
awe. *Re-joice! re-joice! Em - ma - nu-el Shall come to thee, O Is - ra - el.*

ff

* Instrumentation: 2Fl, 2Ob, 2Cl, Bsn, 2Hn, 2Tpt, 2Tbn, B. Tbn, Tba, Timp, Strings. Woodwind, brass and timp are optional if organ is available. Orchestral scores and parts are available

**If this hymn is used processionally, verse 1 may be sung unaccompanied by choir only.

© Oxford University Press 1981. Photocopying this copyright material is ILLEGAL

Printed in Great Britain
OXFORD UNIVERSITY PRESS, MUSIC DEPARTMENT, GREAT CLARENDON STREET, OXFORD OX2 6DP

The Moral Rights of the Arranger have been asserted. Photocopying this copyright material is ILLEGAL

*Congregation sings with tenors and basses.

ff
unis.
Fine
Re -joice! re -joice! Em - ma - nu-el Shall come, O Is - ra - el.
ff
Re - joice! re -joice! Em - ma - nu-el Shall come, O Is - ra - el.
ff
grave. -ry.
Re -joice! re -joice! Em - ma - nu-el Shall come to thee, O Is - ra - el.
Fine
ff
VERSE 3
CHOIR UNACCOMPANIED
p
3. O come, thou Day-spring, come and cheer Our spi-rits by thine ad - vent
p
cresc.
here; Dis-perse the gloo-my clouds of night, And death's dark sha-dows put to
cresc.
D. C. for verse 4
mf
flight. Re -joice! re -joice! Em - ma - nu-el Shall come to thee, O Is - ra - el.
mf

ANGELS WE HAVE HEARD ON HIGH

for Mixed Voices, S. A. T. B., *a cappella*

French traditional carol
arranged by
JOHN RUTTER

© Oxford University Press 1981. Photocopying this copyright material is ILLEGAL

Refrain for Verses 1 and 3

v. 3: rall.
- - - ri-a in ex-cel-sis De - o.
- - - ri - a in ex - cel - sis De - o.
- - - ri-a in ex - cel-sis De - o.
- - - ri - a in ex-cel-sis De - o.
glo - - ri - a in ex-cel-sis De - o.
S.
A.
T.
B.
mp
Glo -
mf
2. Shep-herds, why this ju - bi - lee? Why your joy-ous strains pro-long?
mp
Glo - - ri - a, glo - - ri - a.
mf
Say what may the ti - dings be, Which in-spire your heav'n-ly song?
- - ri - a, glo - ri - a.
2nd Tenors
mf
Glo -

mf
Glo - - - -
- - - - -
mf
Glo - - - -
- ri - a in ex - cel - sis De - o,
- ri - a in ex - cel - sis De - o,
f
- ri - a in ex - cel - sis De - o, Glo -
f
Glo - - - -
f
Glo - - - -
f
Glo - - - -
f
Glo - - - -
- ri - a, glo - ri - a, glo - -

Back to p. 5 for Refrain

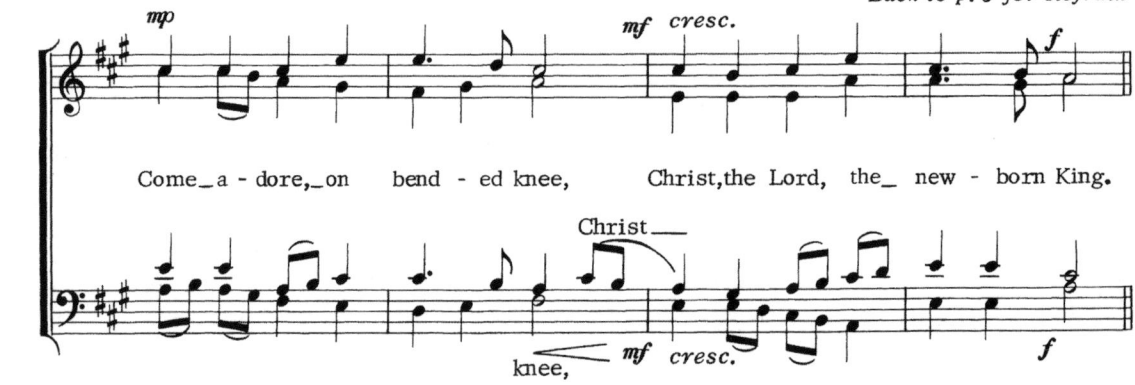

ANGELS, FROM THE REALMS OF GLORY

for Mixed Voices, S. A. T. B., with Organ*

Words by
J. MONTGOMERY

HENRY SMART (1813-1879)
Verse 5 arranged by
JOHN RUTTER

Soprano
Alto

Tenor
Bass

1. An - gels, from the realms of glo - ry, Wing your flight o'er all the earth; Ye who sang cre - a - tion's sto - ry Now pro - claim Mes - si - ah's birth: *Come and wor - ship, come and wor - ship, Wor - ship Christ the new - born King.*

2. Shep-herds, in the field a - bid - ing, Watch-ing o'er your flocks by night, God with man is now re - si - ding; Yon - der shines the in - fant light: *Come and wor - ship, come and wor - ship, Wor - ship Christ the new - born King.*

3. Sages, leave your contemplations;
Brighter visions beam afar;
Seek the great desire of nations;
Ye have seen his natal star:
Come and worship, come and worship,
Worship Christ the new-born King.

4. Saints before the altar bending,
Watching long in hope and fear,
Suddenly the Lord, descending,
In his temple shall appear:
Come and worship, come and worship,
Worship Christ the new-born King.

To next page for verse 5

*Instrumentation: 2Fl, 2Ob, 2Cl, Bsn, 2Hn, 2Tpt, 2Tbn, B. Tbn, Tba, Timp, Strings. Woodwind, brass and timp are optional if organ is available. Orchestral score and parts are available.

© Hinshaw Music, Inc. 1981. Assigned to Oxford University Press 2016. Photocopying this copyright material is ILLEGAL

Descant (Sopranos)
f
5. Though an in - fant now we view him,
All Other Voices
f
5. Though an in - fant now we view him,
Gt. + Sw.
Organ
f
Tuba
Ped.
He shall fill his Fa - ther's throne,
He shall fill his Fa - ther's throne,
Ga - ther all the na - tions to him;
Ga - ther all the na - tions to him;

Ev - 'ry knee shall then bow down:
Ev - 'ry knee shall then bow down:
Gt. + Sw.
ff
Come and wor - ship, come and
ff
Come and wor - ship, come and wor - ship,
ff
Largamente
wor - ship, Come and wor - ship Christ the King.
Wor - ship Christ the new - born King.
Largamente

DING DONG! MERRILY ON HIGH

Words by
G.R. WOODWARD

16th c. French tune
harmonized by CHARLES WOOD

Soprano
Alto
1. Ding dong! mer-ri-ly on high in heav'n the bells are ring-ing:
Ding dong! ve-ri-ly the sky is riv'n with an-gel sing-ing.
2. E'en so here be-low, be-low, let stee-ple bells be swung-en,
And i-o, i-o, i-o, by priest and peo-ple sung-en.
3. Pray you, du-ti-ful-ly prime your mat-in chime, ye ring-ers;
May you beau-ti-ful-ly rime your eve-time song, ye sing-ers.
Tenor
Bass
Glo - - -

WHAT CHILD IS THIS?

for Mixed Voices, S. A. T. B., a cappella

Words by
W. C. DIX

English traditional melody
arranged by JOHN RUTTER

Flowingly (♩. = 50)

Soprano
Solo or Semi-Chorus

Verse 2 only

mp

Aw

S. 1. What child is this, who, laid to rest, On
S. (2.) lies he in such mean es - tate Where

Soprano
Alto

p

A.T.B. 1. *Hum*
A.T.B. (2.) *Aw*
S.A.T.B. (3.) bring him in - cense, gold and myrrh, Come

Hum

Tenor
Bass

p

Aw

(1.) Ma - ry's lap is sleep - ing? Whom an - gels greet with
(2.) ox and ass are feed - ing? Good Chris - tian, fear: for

(1.) Hum
(2.) Aw
(3.) pea - sant, king, to own him, The King of Kings sal -

© Oxford University Press 1981. Photocopying this copyright material is ILLEGAL

Aw
(1.) an - thems sweet, While shep - herds watch are keep - ing?
(2.) sin - ners here The si - lent Word is plead - ing.
(1.) (Hum)
(2.) (Aw)
(3.) - va - tion brings, Let lov - ing hearts en - throne him.
Verses 2 and 3
mf 2. Ah Ah
f 3. This, this is Christ the King, Whom
(1, 2, 3) This, this is Christ the King, Whom
mp (1.) Hum
mf (2.) Ah
f (3.) This, this is Christ the King, Whom
(2.)
(3.) shep - herds guard and an - gels sing:
shep - herds guard and an - gels sing:
(1.) Hum
(2.) Ah
(3.) shep - herds guard and an - gels sing:

(2.) Ah
Ah
(3.) Haste, haste to bring him laud,
The son of
Haste, haste to bring him laud, The babe, the son of
(1.) Hum
(2.) Ah
(3.) Haste, haste to bring him laud, The babe, the son of
1st time
2nd time
2. Why
Ma - ry.
mp
Ma - ry.
mf
(Hum)
Aw
(Ah)
3. So
mp
mf
3rd time
Ma - ry.
p
dim.
pp
Ma - ry.
Hum
p
dim.
pp

GOOD CHRISTIAN MEN, REJOICE

for Mixed Voices, S. A. T. B., with Keyboard*

Words by
J. M. NEALE

German, 14th century
arranged by
JOHN RUTTER

* Instrumentation: 2Fl/Picc, 2Ob, 2Cl, 2Bsn, 2Hn, Perc, Hp, Strings.
Orchestral scores and parts are available.
An unaccompanied arrangement of this melody to the text In dulci jubilo is included in the companion volume, Joy to the World!

© Oxford University Press 1981. Photocopying this copyright material is ILLEGAL

Tenors and Basses
Ox and ass be - fore him bow, And he is in the man - ger now.
All Voices
mf cresc.
f
A
Christ is born to - day!
Christ is born to - day!
f
Soprano
Alto
Tenor
Bass
mf
2. Good Chris - tian men, re - joice With
mf
dim.
p

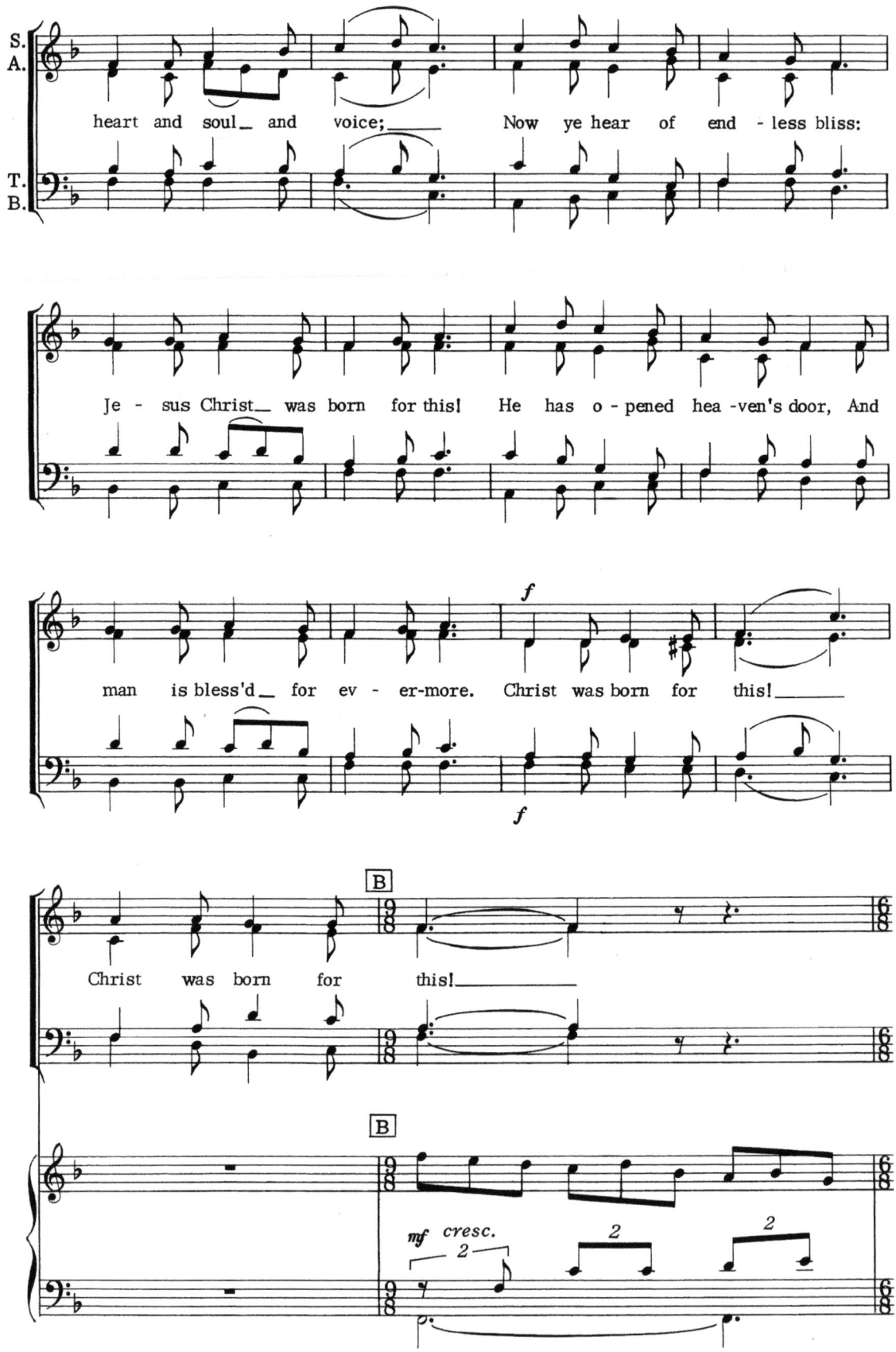
S.
A.
T.
B.
heart and soul and voice; Now ye hear of end - less bliss:
Je - sus Christ was born for this! He has o - pened hea -ven's door, And
man is bless'd for ev - er-more. Christ was born for this!
f
f
B
Christ was born for this!
B
mf cresc.
2
2
2

All Voices
f
3. Good Chris - tian men, re -
f
l.h.
-joice With heart and soul and voice;
S.
A.
Now ye need not fear the grave: Je - sus Christ was born to save!
T.
unis.
B.

ff
Ah
Calls you one and calls you all To gain his e - ver -
unis.
ff
-last - ing hall.
mf
Christ was born to save!
mf
dim.
mf
dim.
rall. al fine
dim.
p
Christ was born to save!
dim.
p
rall. al fine
mf
dim.
p

THE FIRST NOWELL

for Mixed Voices, S. A. T. B., Congregation, with Organ*

English traditional carol

arranged by JOHN RUTTER

Verses 1, 3, and 5
Choir and Congregation

* Instrumentation: 2Fl, 2Ob, 2Cl, Bsn, 2Hn, 2Tpt, 2Tbn, B. Tbn, Tba, Timp, Perc, Strings. Woodwind, brass and percussion are optional if organ is available. Orchestral scores and parts are available.

© Oxford University Press 1981. Photocopying this copyright material is ILLEGAL

Refrain
(all voices)
No - well, No - well, No - well, No -
after v. 1 and 3: straight on
after v. 5: to p. 23
-well, Born is the King of Is - ra - el!
Verses 2 and 4
Choir only
S.
A.
2. They look - ed up and saw a star Shin-ing
4. This star drew nigh to the north - west; O'er
T.
B.
V. 2: organ with voices
V. 4: organ tacet
in the east, be - yond them far; And to the
Beth - le - hem it took its rest, And there it

Refrain
Choir and Congregation

V. 4: organ with voices

Verse 6

Choir 1 and Congregation

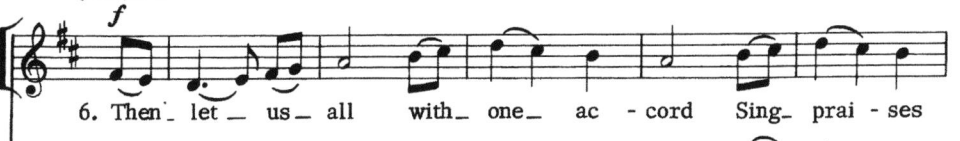

Choir 2 *(optional)*

to our heav'n - ly Lord, That hath made heav'n and
prai-ses
-cord Sing prai - ses to our Lord, That hath made heav'n and
Tuba
earth of naught, And with his blood man - kind hath
earth of naught, And with his blood man - kind hath

Refrain
ff
bought: No - well, No - well, No - well, No - well,
ff
bought: No - well, No - well, No - well, No - well, No -
ff
No - well,
Gt. & Sw.
ff
Born is the King of Is - ra - el!
S. Born is the King of Is - ra - el!
Born is the King of Is - ra - el!
- well, No - well, of Is - ra - el!
Born is the King

AWAY IN A MANGER

Words anon.*

Tune by
J. R. MURRAY
arranged by
JOHN RUTTER

* First published in *A Little Children's Book for Schools and Families* (Lutheran, 1885)

Instrumentation: 2Fl, Hp, Strings. Orchestral scores and parts are available.
An unaccompanied setting of the same text to its original tune by W. J. Kirkpatrick is included in the companion volume Joy to the World!

© Hinshaw Music, Inc. 1981. Assigned to Oxford University Press 2016. Photocopying this copyright material is ILLEGAL

down where he lay, The lit - tle Lord Je - sus a - sleep on the
S.
A.
hay.
unis. mp
T.
B.
2. The
A
p
Aw
Aw
cat - tle are low - ing, the ba - by a - wakes, But lit - tle Lord
A

Aw
poco cresc.
Je - sus no cry - ing he makes. I love thee, Lord Je - sus! Look
Aw
dim.
down from the sky, And stay by my side un - til morn - ing is nigh.
B
pp soft and gentle
3. Be near me, Lord
3. Be near
pp soft and gentle
B
dim.
p
pp

poco cresc.
Je - sus, me, I ask thee to stay Close by me for ev - er, and
poco cresc.
p
love me, I pray. Bless all the dear chil - dren in thy ten - der
p
B. 2 Bless all in thy ten - der
Slower
pp
care, And fit us for hea - ven, to live with thee there.
pp
care,
Slower
pp
p
dim.
pp

O HOLY NIGHT

(Cantique de Noël)

for Mixed Voices, S. A. T. B., with Organ*

Words by
CAPPEAU DE ROQUEMAURE

ADOLPHE ADAM (1803-1856)
arranged by JOHN RUTTER

*Instrumentation: 2Fl, Ob, 2Cl, Bsn, 2Hn, Hp, Strings. Orchestral scores and parts are available.
**Soprano part in verse 1 may be sung by a solo soprano or tenor.

© Hinshaw Music, Inc. 1981. Assigned to Oxford University Press 2016. Photocopying this copyright material is ILLEGAL

night of the dear Sa - vior's birth;
Dieu des - cen - dit jus - qu'à nous,
Long lay the world in sin and er - ror
Pour ef - fa - cer la tache o - ri - gi -
pin - ing, Till he ap - peared, and the soul felt its
-nel - le Et de son Père ar - rê - ter le cour -

worth. A thrill of hope the
-roux. Le monde en - tier tres -
mf
mp
mp
cresc.
mp
wea - ry world re - joic - es, For yon - der breaks a
-sail - le d'es - pé - ran - ce A cet - te nuit qui
cresc.
cresc.
new and glo - rious morn.
lui donne un Sau - veur.
A Fall on your
Peu - - ple, à ge -
f
mf
Ah
mf
A
mf

knees! Oh hear the an-gel voi - ces! O
-noux! at - tends ta dé-li - vran - ce. No-
Ah
night di - vine! O night when Christ was
-ël! No - ël! voi - ci le Ré-demp-
O night di - vine! O night when Christ was
No - ël! No - ël! Voi - ci le Ré - demp -
born, O night di - vine,
-teur, No - ël! No - ël!
cresc.
born, O night di - vine, O
-teur, No - ël! No - ël! le
cresc.
born, O night di - vine,
-teur, No - ël! No - ël!

O night di - vine.
-demp - - - - teur.
dim.
night di - vine.
Ré - demp - teur.
dim.
mp
B
unis. mf
2. Led by the
2. De no - tre
tr
B
Sw.
mp
Ah
light of faith se-rene - ly beam - ing, With glow - ing
foi que la lu-miè - re ar - den - te Nous gui - de

Ah
by his cra - dle we
au ber-ceau de l'en-
div.
hearts by his cra - dle we stand;
tous au ber-ceau de l'en - fant,
stand.
-fant.
Ah
unis.
So, led by light of a star sweet - ly
Comme au - tre - fois une é - toi - le bril -
Ah
div.
gleam - ing, Here came the wise men from the O - rient
-lan - te Y con - dui - sit les chefs de l'o - ri-

p
the O - rient land. The King of Kings
de l'o - ri - ent. Le Roi des Rois
p
unis.
land. The King of Kings lay
-ent. Le Roi des Rois naît
p
cresc.
lay in low - ly man - ger,
dans une hum - ble crè - che, puis -
cresc.
thus in low - ly man - ger, In all our tri - als
dans une hum - ble crè - che; Puis - sants du jour, fiers
cresc.
C
mf
born our friend.
- sants du jour.
f
Ah
born to be our friend; He knows our
de vo-tre grand-eur, A vo - tre or-
C
mf

Ah
Ah
div.
need, to our weak - ness no
-geuil c'est de là qu'un Dieu
Ah
f
Be - hold, be -
Cour - bez, cour -
stran - ger; Be - hold your
prê - che; Cour - bez vos
dim.
mf
- hold your King! be - fore him
- bez vos fronts de - vant le Ré - demp -
unis.
mf
King! dim. be - fore him low - ly
fronts de - vant le Ré - demp -

cresc.
bend! Be - hold your King, be - hold your
-teur, Cour-bez vos fronts, cour-bez vos
bend! Be - hold your
-teur, Cour - bez vos
cresc.
cresc.
f
mp
King! be - fore him
fronts, le Ré - demp -
f King! your King! dim. be - fore him
fronts de - vant le Ré - demp -
f
dim.
mp
bend!
-teur.
bend!
-teur.
Gt. Fls. 8', 4'
2
2
2
2

D
mp
cresc.
3. Tru - ly he taught us to love one an -
3. Le Ré-demp - teur a bri - sé toute en-
mp
cresc.
tr
D
(Gt. Fls.)
(mp)
mf
- oth - er; His law is love and his Gos - pel is
- tra - ve, La terre est li - bre et le ciel est ou -
mf
cresc.
peace.
Chains shall he break, for the slave is our
- vert.
Il voit un frère où n'é - tait qu'un es-
cresc.
cresc.

f
mf
bro - ther, And in his Name all op - pres - sion shall
-cla - ve, L'a-mour u - nit ceux qu'en-chaî - nait le
f
mf
mf
mf
cease. Sweet hymns of joy in
fer. Qui lui di - ra no -
mf
mp
cresc.
grate - ful cho - rus raise we, Let all with - in us
-tre re - con - nais - san - ce? C'est pour nous tous qu'il
cresc.

E
f
praise his ho - ly Name. Christ is the
naît, qu'il souf-fre et meurt. Peu - - ple, de-
f
E
mf
Lord, then ev - er, ev -er praise we, His
-bout, chan - te ta dé - li - vran - ce, No-
and glo - ry ev - er-more pro -
No - ël! chan - tons le Ré-demp-
pow'r and glo - ry ev - er - more pro -
-ël! No - ël! No - ël! No - ël! No -
2
and glo - ry ev - er - more pro -
No - ël! No - ël, chan-tons No -

-claim, His pow'r and glo - - - ry
-teur, No - ël! No - ël! chan -
cresc.
ff
-claim, His pow'r and glo - ry ev - er,
-ël! No - ël! No - ël! No - ël! chan -
-claim!
-ël!
cresc.
ff
cresc.
f
ev - er - more pro - claim.
-tons le Ré - demp - teur.
(Gt.)
(f)
Gt.
tr
Sw.
mf rit.
dim.
p

JOY TO THE WORLD!

(original version)

Words by ISAAC WATTS

LOWELL MASON (1792-1872)
based on HANDEL

Soprano
Alto

1. Joy to the world! the Lord is come: Let earth re-ceive her
2. Joy to the earth! the Sa-vior reigns: Let men their songs em-

Tenor
Bass

King; Let ev-'ry heart pre-pare him room, And
-ploy; While fields and floods, rocks, hills, and plains Re-

heav'n and na-ture sing, And heav'n and na-ture sing, And
-peat the sound-ing joy, Re-peat the sound-ing joy, Re-

And heav'n and na-ture sing, And heav'n and na-ture
Re-peat the sound-ing joy, Re-peat the sound-ing

heav'n, and heav'n and na-ture sing.
-peat, re-peat the sound-ing joy.

sing, And heav'n and na-ture sing.
joy, Re-peat the sound-ing joy.

3. No more let sins and sorrows grow,
Nor thorns infest the ground;
He comes to make his blessings flow
Far as the curse is found.

4. He rules the world with truth and grace;
And makes the nations prove
The glories of his righteousness
And wonders of his love.

An accompanied arrangement of this hymn, for choir, is included in the companion volume, Joy to the World!

© Hinshaw Music, Inc. 1981. Assigned to Oxford University Press 2016. Photocopying this copyright material is ILLEGAL

THREE KINGS OF ORIENT

(unaccompanied version)

for Mixed Voices, S. A. T. B.

Words and Music by
J. H. HOPKINS
arranged by JOHN RUTTER

An accompanied arrangement of this carol is included in the companion volume, Joy to the World!

© Oxford University Press 1981. Photocopying this copyright material is ILLEGAL

*If desired, choir may hum the parts of verse 5 during the singing of verses 2 and 3. Verse 4 should be sung unaccompanied, an octave lower than verses 2 and 3.

GO, TELL IT ON THE MOUNTAIN

for Mixed Voices, S. A. T. B., with Piano*

American folk song
arranged by JOHN RUTTER

NOTE: This melody exists in several variant versions. As far as can be ascertained, none of them is definitive, so the present version has been chosen from personal preference.

*Instrumentation: 2Fl, 2Ob, 2Cl, 2Bsn, 2Hn, Timp, Perc, Pno (optional), Hp, Strings. Orchestral scores and parts are available.

© Oxford University Press 1981. Photocopying this copyright material is ILLEGAL

A
mf
Go, tell it on the moun - tain, O-ver the hills and
A
mf
ev - 'ry - where. Go, tell it on the moun - tain That
Faster, in 2; freely
mp
Je - sus Christ is born.
1. While
mp
Faster, in 2; freely
dim.
Ped.

* If preferred, tenors may sing in unison with basses for the next eight measures.

ev - 'ry - where. Go, tell it on the moun - tain That
Je - sus Christ is born.
mp
2. The shep-herds feared and
dim.
mp
mp
cresc.
When lo, a-bove the earth
cresc.
trem - bled When lo, a - bove the earth Rang
f
cresc.

f
poco rall.
dim.
Rang out the cho-rus, Hail his birth!
out the an - gel cho - rus That hailed our Sa-vior's birth.
dim.
poco rall.
f
dim.
C a tempo
mp legato, poco dolce
cresc.
Go, tell it on the moun - tain, O-ver the hills and
mp legato, poco dolce
cresc.
C a tempo
mp
cresc.
mf
ev - 'ry - where. Go, tell it on the moun - tain That
mf
moun - tain
mf

mp
Je - sus Christ_ is born. 3. Down in a low - ly
mp
dim.
mp
man - ger The hum - ble Christ was born, And
mp
Ped.
poco rall.
p
brought us God's sal - va - tion That bless - ed Christ - mas morn.
p
poco rall.
p

D a tempo
accel.
cresc.
div.
mf cresc.
Go, tell it on the moun-tain, O-ver the hills and
div.
cresc.
Go, tell it on the moun - tain,
mf cresc.
D a tempo
accel.
cresc.
mf cresc.
f
cresc.
ev - 'ry where. Go, tell it on the moun - tain That
f
cresc.
f
cresc.
allargando
a tempo - vivace (♩ = 144)
ff
Je - sus Christ is born.
ff
allargando
a tempo - vivace (♩ = 144)
ff

dim.
rall. poco a poco
p
That
Go, tell it on the moun - tain
mp
dim.
p
rall. poco a poco
mp
dim.
p
Lento al fine
dim.
pp
Je - sus
Je - sus
Christ is
born.
p
dim.
pp
Lento al fine
p
dim.
pp

HARK! THE HERALD ANGELS SING

for Mixed Voices, S. A. T. B., with Organ*

Words by C. WESLEY
T. WHITEFIELD, M. MADAN
and others

MENDELSSOHN
Verse 3 arranged by
JOHN RUTTER

Soprano
Alto
(Organ)
Tenor
Bass

f 1. Hark! the he - rald an - gels sing Glo - ry to the new-born King;
mf 2. Christ, by high - est heav'n a - dored, Christ, the e - ver - last - ing Lord,

Peace on earth and mer - cy mild, God and sin - ners re - con-ciled:
Late in time be - hold him come Off-spring of a vir-gin's womb:

Joy - ful all ye na - tions rise, Join the tri - umph of the skies,
Veiled in flesh the God-head see, Hail th'in - car - nate De - i - ty!

With th'an - gel - ic host pro-claim, Christ is born in Beth - le - hem.
Pleased as man with man to dwell, Je - sus our Em - ma - nu - el.

Org.

Hark! the he-rald an - gels sing Glo - ry to the new-born King.

Org. ped.

Melody and harmony for verses 1 and 2 adapted by W. H. Cummings (1831-1915) from a chorus by Mendelssohn.

*Instrumentation: 2Fl, 2Ob, 2Cl, 2Bsn, 2Hn, 2Tpt, 2Tbn, B. Tbn, Tba, Timp, Perc, Strings. Woodwind, brass and percussion are optional if organ is available. Orchestral scores and parts are available.

© Hinshaw Music, Inc. 1981. Assigned to Oxford University Press 2016. Photocopying this copyright material is ILLEGAL

Descant (Sopranos)
3. Hail the heav'n - born Prince of Peace! Hail the Sun of
All other voices
3. Hail the heav'n - born Prince of Peace! Hail the Sun of Right-eous-ness!
Right-eous-ness! Light and life to all,
Light and life to all he brings, Ris'n with heal - ing
to all he brings, Mild he lays his glo - ry by,
in his wings; Mild he lays his glo - ry by,

Printed by Halstan

A SERVICE OF READINGS AND CAROLS

OPENING HYMN *O come, O come, Emmanuel*

BIDDING PRAYER *(spoken by the Minister)*

Beloved in Christ, be it at this Christmas-tide our care and delight to hear again the message of the angels, and in heart and mind to go even unto Bethlehem and see this thing which is come to pass, and the Babe lying in a manger.

Therefore let us read and mark in Holy Scripture the tale of the loving purposes of God and the glorious redemption brought us by this Holy Child.

But first, let us pray for the needs of the whole world; for peace on earth and goodwill among all his people; for unity and brotherhood within the Church he came to build, and especially in this our congregation.

And because this would rejoice his heart, let us remember, in his name, the poor and helpless, the cold, the hungry, and the oppressed; the sick and them that mourn, the lonely and the unloved, the aged and the little children; all those who know not the Lord Jesus, or who love him not, or who by sin have grieved his heart of love.

Lastly, let us remember before God all those who rejoice with us, but upon another shore, and in a greater light, that multitude which no man can number, whose hope was in the Word made flesh, and with whom in this Lord Jesus we for evermore are one.

These prayers and praises let us humbly offer up to the throne of heaven, in the words which Christ himself hath taught us:

THE LORD'S PRAYER *(spoken by all)*

CAROL *Angels we have heard on high*

HYMN *Angels, from the realms of glory*

READING St Matthew 1, vv. 18-23

CAROLS *Ding dong! merrily on high*
What child is this?
Good Christian men, rejoice

HYMN *The first Nowell*

READING St Luke 2, vv. 8-16

CAROLS *Away in a manger*
O holy night

HYMN *Joy to the world!*

READING St Matthew 2, vv. 1-11

CAROLS *Three kings of Orient*
Go, tell it on the mountain

READING St John 1, vv. 1-14

Minister The Lord be with you
Congregation And with thy spirit
Minister Let us pray

THE COLLECT FOR CHRISTMAS EVE *(spoken by the Minister)*

O God, who makest us glad with the yearly remembrance of the birth of thy only Son, Jesus Christ: Grant that as we joyfully receive him for our Redeemer, so we may with sure confidence behold him, when he shall come to be our judge; who liveth and reigneth with thee and the Holy Spirit, one God, world without end. *Amen.*

THE BLESSING *(spoken by the Minister)*

May he who by his Incarnation gathered into one things earthly and heavenly, fill you with the sweetness of inward peace and goodwill; and the blessing of God Almighty, the Father, the Son, and the Holy Spirit, be upon you and remain with you always. *Amen.*

CLOSING HYMN *Hark! the herald angels sing*